Network Marketing Step by Step:

How anyone (from business leadership to introverts) can make money and achieve success by becoming a social media network marketing pro

By Ray Worre

Table of Contents

9781798831984

Introduction

Chapter 1: Intro to Network Marketing

Why Choose Network Marketing?

Is Network Marketing a Scam?

Success Stories

Sarah Robbins
Ray Higdon
Donna Johnson
Mike Sims

How to Make Big Bucks

Chapter 2: Choosing the Right Company

Finding a Company that You Believe In

The Importance of a Mission Statement

Customer and Consultant Testimonials

Considering the Commission Structure

Consider the Team You Want to Join

Making Your Decision

Chapter 3: Committing to the Idea
Taking Responsibility for Your Success
Learning to Make Your Own Opportunities
Seeking Help from Your Upline
Learning from Industry Leaders

Chapter 4: Finding Prospects
Always Be on the Lookout
Use Success Stories to Sell
Leveraging Social Media and Email
Gauging Your Audience

Chapter 5: Presenting to Prospects
Selling from Small to Large
Accepting the Word "No"
Upselling Your Clients
Closing Sales

Chapter 6: The Follow-Up
Timing Your Follow Up
Organizing Your Follow-Up System
Effective Follow-Up Strategies

Chapter 7: Promoting Products and Events
Branding Yourself

Video Marketing Strategies

Targeted Content Curation

Attending the Right Events

Showing Products in Use

Chapter 8: Handling Rejection

Understanding the Difference Between Objection and Rejection

Respecting When No Means No

Making Rejection Easier To Manage

Put it into Perspective
Detaching from the Outcome
Asking for a Reason
Avoiding Emotional Attachment

Chapter 9: A Winning Mindset

Self-Discipline

Mental Toughness

Staying Self-Motivated

Stay Curious

Monitor Your Thoughts

Chapter 10: Future of Network Marketing

Conclusion

Introduction

Message from the authors:

The best virtue to have when you are trying to build a business is patience. If you can't learn to take your time and enjoy the process, you will never get to where you want to be. The Step-by-step series will help you apply this way of thought and teach you how to follow it in every book we write. We will show you how to break down your business idea into simple and easy to follow steps. By dividing the process into short sections we give you the opportunity to be able to visualize a clear goal and have the skills in order to get where you want to be in your business ventures.Our commitment to making your business dreams come true will always be there, but it is your job to start yourself on the right path. By buying this book you have taken your first step. Good luck

Congratulations on downloading *Network Marketing Success!*

Network marketing is a powerful business opportunity that enables individuals who are interested in working from home or working remotely to take control of their finances and live their best lives. Did you know that the network marketing industry has produced more millionaires than any other industry there is? Network marketing truly has the capacity to change lives, financially, socially, and often through the products that are being shared as well.

Since you are here, I can assume that you have the desire to learn how to enter network marketing, or how to grow your network marketing business so that you can begin experiencing the success that this industry is known for helping people create. Chances are, you have seen someone you know or admire, climb the ranks of network marketing and completely change their lives, their families' lives, and the lives of their team members in massive ways. Aside from positive financial changes, network marketing often provides people with unexpected yet equally phenomenal social changes as well, as many people begin to feel far more supported and connected by their network marketing community than they ever dreamed possible.

These days, network marketing is amidst a major shift as marketers are learning how to adapt to the ever-evolving world of online business and marketing. Unfortunately, many people are still sharing outdated information on how to market your products, handle sales calls, and increase your income through the network marketing business model. This information may have worked in the past, but in modern network marketing models, it often leads to alienation, embarrassment, and disappointingly low growth rates in your business. Naturally, you do not want to endure any of these challenges of network marketing; you want to experience the same joy, pride, and excitement that the top income earners in the industry are experiencing! That is exactly what you are about to learn, too. As you dive into the chapters of this book, you will discover that network marketing can be made extremely simple and can provide many positive benefits and experiences for you and your family.

The strategies that you are about to learn are positive, inspiring, and effective at helping you not only to launch your business but generate massive success along the way as well. If you are ready to begin your successful network marketing business that brings you profit and pride, then without further ado, let's begin!

Chapter 1: Intro to Network Marketing

Network marketing is a popular peer to peer business model where consultants of various companies build their networks and market products to their respective networks. As each consultant brings on new customers or consultants for the company, they are compensated for this, thus allowing them to generate a profit from their network of contacts. Network marketing companies are modeled in a way where a company decides to develop products or services and then hires several consultants to market those products or services to bring on clients. Each consultant is a contracted worker, not an employee, which means that they essentially own their own business and are responsible for generating their own income.

This business model has existed for nearly a hundred years now, with the first company being launched in the early 1900s. Since its development, network marketing has seen many shifts and changes in terms of how the companies are designed, how consultants are paid, and how their products are delivered. However, the basic model of the company has always remained the same; the company produces the goods or services, the consultants market them, and then the consumers buy them.

Why Choose Network Marketing?

Network marketing is one of the easiest home-based businesses to build, especially in our modern world where we have access to the internet and a global opportunity to build our networks. If you have ever dreamed of being self-employed, setting your own schedule, staying home with your family or traveling the world, or otherwise having a significant amount of control over your time and freedom, then network marketing is a powerful opportunity for you. Because of how this business model is structured and because of our access to social media marketing, network marketing can be leveraged to help you generate a massive profit from the comforts of your own remote locations.

Aside from giving you plenty of time freedom and flexibility, network marketing also offers one additional significant resource that people greatly value. That resource is cash or, more importantly, financial freedom, which allows you the opportunity to make virtually any decision you desire in your life and have the financial assets to back up that decision. Network marketing is built in a way that enables people to generate residual income off of their team members since you are paid a percentage from all of your active downline members. This means that because of network marketing's standard commission's model, you are able to generate a percentage of commissions from your own customers, as well as a percentage of your recruit's commissions based off of their sales.

Many individuals enter this company and develop their teams in a way that allows them to no longer feel the need to contribute to working for the company anymore because their teams have grown so massively. Instead, they allow their team members to do the work or they enjoy minimal involvement by offering live trainings and guidance on how to grow and leave the rest of the one-on-one guidance up to their team members.

Having the capacity to generate a team so massive that you earn five figure or six figure monthly paychecks is something that most people would never dream to be possible until they are introduced to the world of network marketing. Upon discovering the model, however, many people will leverage it and start earning a significant income off of their network marketing business that enables them to enjoy time and financial freedom, thus giving them the resources they need to live the lives they truly desire to live.

Is Network Marketing a Scam?

For years, people have claimed that network marketing is a scam or a pyramid scheme that will never benefit anyone except those who sit at the top. This false information has led to many individuals being unwilling to join or afraid to develop their own businesses for fear of being seen as frauds or scammers by their own friends. Fortunately, this information is not true and you can rest assured that network marketing is no more of a pyramid scheme than any standard business model is. Think of it this way: if you were to receive a job at a local office building, there would likely be one boss, one general manager, one assistant manager, a few team leaders, and several employees. This is a pyramid-shaped business model that has a few people at the top earning healthy salaries and growing wealthy while the rest of the company is earning average wages and may or may not be struggling to get ahead financially.

True pyramid schemes or Ponzi schemes as they are otherwise known as are designed in a way where only the people at the top benefit and others always lose. In true Ponzi scheme situations, everyone is lead to believe that they will earn some form of income or earnings but there will be several at the bottom who will never earn anything. In network marketing models, everyone is offered a fair opportunity to create an income through their business and there are several people who will only purchase through the company as customers with no intention to become consultants. These customers are then at the "bottom" of the pyramid and they are not earning anything, not because they are being cheated out of money, but because they are not interested in taking up the business opportunity to make money in the first place.

Many people believe that there will always be consultants in network marketing who fail because the majority of people who join are in one way or another being set up for failure. This is another myth that commonly causes people to object to the idea of joining a network marketing business for fear of being one of those people who is going to be set up to fail just so that consultants above them can succeed. The reality is: in any business or commissions based position, people who are not prepared to take action and educate themselves on how to leverage the opportunity are not going to make money. This is true whether you are in car sales, real estate, starting your own business from scratch, or network marketing. If you are not ready to educate yourself on how to build a proper network, market to them effectively, sell them your products, and recruit them to your team, you will not generate money from this business model. This is not because it is a scam like many people will claim it to be, but because it is an opportunity that requires time, attention, and education in order to grow it. While the process of growing your network marketing business and generating a passive income is flexible, it does still come with a learning curve that will require you to first take the time to understand how to leverage the model, *then* make the big bucks.

So, to summarize — no, network marketing is not a scam or a pyramid scheme. It is a viable way for many people to make a large amount of money with a successful work at home business model. The people who are calling it a scam have either not taken the time to educate themselves on what a network marketing company actually is, or they have tried it out and failed to learn how to leverage it properly so they decided it must be a problem with the business model and not them.

Success Stories

There are thousands of network marketing and MLM (multi-level marketing) success stories available to read on the internet, but a few of them are particularly noteworthy and worth paying attention to. The following success stories are great testaments to how any person from any background can join network marketing and generate success with their opportunity if they desire to do so.

Sarah Robbins

Sarah Robbins was initially a teacher who feared that she may lose her job due to the unstable economy that she was working at the time. When she was introduced to Rodan and Fields, she decided it would be a fun way to earn an extra income and allow her to have some extra money to spend each month, particularly during months where finances were more challenging. Early on, Robbins realized she was onto something and began growing her Rodan and Fields business to the point where she was able to begin earning six figures every single month through her network marketing business. She left her teaching career behind when she matched her salary and then quickly exceeded it, which allowed her to have more freedom to do the things she enjoyed and less fear around what might happen if the rocky economy finally swallowed up her career.

Robbins was actually the first consultant ever to be conducted into the Rodan and Fields Hall of Fame, and she also became the first consultant to reach the Million Dollar Circle within the company. To this day, she continues to be the top-selling consultant within the company, earning a high six figure per month income through her Rodan and Fields marketing business.

Ray Higdon

Unlike Robbins, Ray Higdon was actually a victim of the 2008 recession when several of his financial investments went bust and his marriage went up in flames.

Higdon lost his properties, his finances, and his wife through a difficult divorce all in one go, which left him with virtually nothing. Sometime after his major loss, Higdon met and began dating a girl named Jessica who introduced him to Numis and encouraged him to join the team. By February 2011, just three years after his 2008 losses, Higdon broke company records and earned a record of $46,000 in a single month, which at the time, was the highest anyone had ever earned in a single month with the company. By June of that same year, Higdon had earned more than $52,000 in income that month and continued to grow that earning income to record heights month after month. Nowadays, Higdon is not quite as involved in the sales of the company but instead spends his time training other network marketers to generate success in their own business opportunities by offering them tips, guidance, and trainings to succeed with network marketing.

Donna Johnson

Donna Johnson started out as someone who did not believe that she could generate a positive life for herself or her family because she felt that she was in a position that would prevent her from being able to do so. Johnson did not have a college degree and worked as a single mother teaching other children how to swim. When Johnson was introduced to the company Arbonne, she thought that this may be her winning opportunity to change the story for herself and her family and start creating a positive impact on her network. Nearly 40 years later, Johnson is still with Arbonne and earns more than $1 million per year as one of the top leaders in the company, and also earns a free white Mercedes to drive.

Since she was able to spin her own luck and start generating such massive success for her own family, Johnson decided to take some of her earnings and invest them into projects that allow her to give back to others. Johnson owns a popular bed and breakfast in Jamaica and regularly donates to organizations that help orphans and the less fortunate.

Mike Sims

Mike Sims was originally from Alabama where he attended Auburn University and began working in the finance industry. Sims quickly discovered that he was highly ambitious and that working at a desk job from 9 to 5 was not fulfilling for him or his ambitions. Unlike other network marketers who only go on to succeed in one company, Sims decided to start two and simultaneously built both of them up to incredible levels of success. He became a top earner in each company, where he started earning a seven figure income between the two of them. Sims received multiple awards and achievement ranks through both companies before going on to launch his own company, Mike Sims Worldwide.

How to Make Big Bucks

Obviously, network marketing has the potential to help people make a massive income from this business model if they leverage it effectively. That being said, if you are not leveraging the model effectively, the chances of you generating success with network marketing are rather slim. In the remaining chapters of this book, you are going to be shown how you can maximize your earnings with network marketing and start generating high six and seven figure incomes with consistent business growth. Before we get started, however, I want to let you in on the three things that it takes to be successful in network marketing: the right opportunity, the right marketing strategy, and the right mindset. When you get started in network marketing, if you are not backed by the right opportunity, you are going to struggle to grow because you simply will not have the products, services, or company to back you up and help you succeed. You also need to make sure that you are staying up to date on the latest marketing trends and serving in a way that allows people to want to see and engage with you and your products, to avoid alienating yourself and driving your audience away. Finally, you need to make sure that you are regularly working toward developing your mindset and creating a mind that is set for success so that when you face obstacles, hurdles, or hardships in your business, you are mentally prepared to overcome them, no matter what. As any successful business owner will tell you, running a business comes with a lot of challenges and trying moments, and you need to be ready to endure those moments and have the mental strength and resiliency to carry forward even if it feels particularly challenging to do so. The rewards in the end will always pay off, but there is no guarantee that the journey there will be easy, and anyone who tells you that it is always easy all the time is kidding themselves, and you.

Chapter 2: Choosing the Right Company

When it comes to network marketing, the company that you are with can make all the difference in your ability to generate positive opportunities and a healthy income or not. Being involved with a company that you love, a team that you can grow with, and a commission structure that you can leverage is important if you are going to be able to turn your side hustle into a real multiple six or seven figure income. If you have already started with a company and you are reading this book to learn how to leverage your opportunity more, you should still take the time to read through this chapter to ensure that you really have chosen an opportunity that you can grow with. If you have not, this chapter is going to support you in deciding which company will provide you with the best platform to leverage the network marketing model so that you can earn a high income.

Remember, when it comes to network marketing, not every opportunity is the same and not all businesses are going to be as easy to leverage. Regardless of what anyone may say about whether or not your network marketing company is "really a business that you own," you need to treat it like it is a business that you own or you are going to struggle to generate success. When it comes to marketing, building a team, and creating opportunities for yourself, you lead your business like a real business, which means that you need to make decisions like a real business owner. Part of making decisions like a real business owner is learning how to spot effective opportunities that you can leverage so that you can earn a higher income through your company. If you do not already have experience with making big decisions such as this, worry not, everything in this chapter will show you exactly what you need to know to succeed.

Finding a Company that You Believe In

The very first thing that you need to look for when it comes to choosing which company you want to join is picking a company that you can actually believe in. If you are not with a company that you genuinely believe in, you are going to struggle to market it to anyone because you are not going to feel authentic and honest when you share it with the people in your network. The easiest way to find a company that you believe in is to start by identifying what your hobbies and interests are and seek out companies that are going to effectively align with your interests. When you find a company that sells products or services you are passionate about, believing in what they have to offer is significantly easier because they are clearly aligned with things that you enjoy.

Once you have identified what you are passionate about and discovered some companies that align with these passions, start looking through their websites to see if you can find information that stands out to you or draws your interest. Often, this simple visual check is a great way to see whether or not a company visually aligns with you, as you are going to want to choose a company that has a platform that makes sense to you and feels good to you. Chances are if you land on the website and feel put off or disinterested, your clients will feel the same way, which means that this may not be the best opportunity for you to connect with people and share your products.

The Importance of a Mission Statement

The next thing you need to look at with your potential companies is what their mission statements are, or the values that they share on their website. Every company will make a mission statement and, in one way or another, will share their values with their audience through their platform. Taking the time to find these mission statements or values and determining whether or not they align with your own values and mission is important, as this is a large part of deciding whether or not you can completely get behind the company that you are considering selling for.

If the mission statement or values of the company are not made clear on their website, take some time to browse through the company's story and any additional pages that may give you insight as to what the company stands for. Typically, you can gain a fairly clear image into what a company stands for by paying attention to what words they use, what causes they highlight, and what main points they try to nurture with their audience.

Customer and Consultant Testimonials

When you are looking to join a company, you should always look beyond the company to learn more about it as well. A company can say anything they desire about themselves, but the people who have experience with them will have a more intimate understanding with a perception that closely matches the one that you need to look into to determine whether or not this opportunity will fit with you. You can find customer and consultant testimonials in many different ways, though there are typically two ways that you want to look for them. First, if you personally know a consultant, ask them to provide you with some testimonials, and if possible, to introduce you to their customers. Typically, a consultant who is proud of their work and their company will be able to put you in touch with other consultants or customers who have had experience with the company that can help answer any questions that you may have and give you some feedback on the company.

When you communicate with other people about the company you are considering, you have the opportunity to see how passionate people are, how supportive the community is, and whether or not the products are actually as high quality as they claim to be. This is also a great opportunity for you to start getting a feel for how comfortable it is to talk about the products with other people so that you can determine whether or not this is something you want to continue talking about on an ongoing basis. Remember, this is something you want to be able to do for the long haul, so you need to be prepared to choose a company that offers products and services that you enjoy talking about so that as you reach out into your network and start sharing, it is an enjoyable experience.

Considering the Commission Structure

The primary reason for launching a network marketing business is to get paid, so naturally, you want to pay attention to the compensation plan being offered by the companies that you are considering. At first, any network marketing compensation plan can seem confusing as they are typically structured in a way that is unlike what any other payment structure you have likely seen before, so it may be useful to have someone go over the basic structure with you to help you understand it. If you are unsure of who you can reach out to, or if you are feeling confused by other peoples' explanations, searching for a YouTube video that outlines basic network marketing commission structures is a useful way to determine what these compensation plans typically look like.

It is important that once you understand the general payment structure, you audit all potential companies to see if they have a strong payment structure or a weak one. Every company creates their payment structure in a slightly different way and will typically offer unique bonuses as well, so make sure that you take the time to look over each company's plan to see which one fits your needs the best. Ideally, you should join a company that offers the opportunity to start making as much money as possible right away so that you can begin seeing the benefits of your investments early on.

Although there is no set structure or standard to determine what constitutes as a good payment plan and what doesn't, you can always look into each plan and compare what they have to offer and how they are setting you up to earn an income through their company. While you will not want to make your entire decision based solely on the compensation plan of any given company, knowing that you are considering only those companies that are going to set you up for success is a great way to ensure that you are joining the right one. That being said, you will need to determine what works best for you in regards to what bonuses you want to earn, what commissions seem the most sustainable, and which one seems to offer the ranks that are the most achievable.

Consider the Team You Want to Join

When you join a network marketing company, you join a team of people who are already selling for the said company which ultimately puts you into a paid position in their network. This team, or network, is responsible for educating you on your products, guiding you through the process of launching your business and marketing your products, and helping you create success. You will be spending a lot of time working together, supporting each other, and cheering each other on with developing your businesses, earning your income, and growing your collective network. Because this network is going to be such a big part of your journey, it is important that you pay attention to who exists in the network and how they are going to be able to support you in generating the success that you desire to create with your company.

The first thing that you want to look at when it comes to your potential team is the top earners who exist on your network marketing team. The top earners on your team are going to tell you a lot about what type of team you are joining, what the company can offer you, and where the average cap is for top income earners. You want to join a company where the top income earners are making a positive living, are portrayed by a diverse team of people from all different backgrounds, and are readily available to and willing to support their downlines in generating success as well. Aside from the top earners, you also want to look at the general team that you will be joining to see what the energy is like in the team and whether or not it suits your needs. Look for a team that is going to offer you diversity in its members and open support. If you start to notice any clique-like behaviors, a lack of support from the upline of the group, or a dominant theme of outdated marketing strategies and competitiveness existing within the group, it may not be a productive one for you to grow in.

Ideally, you want a team that is going to be open, warm, and inviting. You should be able to feel confident in making new friends on your team, being supported in understanding how the company works, and feel as though you are going to have individuals there to help walk you through the early stages. Of course, over time, you will not need as much support because you will understand how the company works and you will be able to start leading other downline members in the team the way that you were lead, but early on, this abundance of support and guidance can make a world of difference. If you truly want to succeed, you are going to want to know that you have positioned yourself in a team where there are other people that are prepared to help you succeed as well.

Making Your Decision

As you can probably tell, making the decision of which company you are going to join is vital as you want to make sure that you join a company that is going to help position you for success. If you have done your research effectively until now, you should have enough information to look through your options and get a feel for where you are going to fit in best. Part of your decision is going to be made on your gut feeling, as you will likely have a general feeling of which company is going to offer you everything that you are looking for and support you in generating success with this business model. That being said, relying on a gut feeling alone is often not reason enough to proceed with any major business decision because you will need to bring in logic and reason to make sure that you are making the right decision for the long haul.

The easiest way to determine what company you are going to join is to take a piece of paper and write down everything that you know about each of the companies that you have researched so far. Make sure that you highlight the information that stands out to you as positive, as well as the information that stands out to you as possibly being negative, as you want to be very clear about both sides of what you are looking at. Once you have written everything down, cross off any of the companies that clearly do not match the others, if there are any. The companies you want to cross off would be companies that have overly complex or underwhelming compensation plans, that have a very unwelcoming or uncomfortable team vibe, or that do not have much diversity existing at the top of their teams.

Once you have your final two or three companies to compare, all you need to do is decide which one feels the best for you and offers everything that you are looking for. Remember, how you feel about the company and what it offers you are extremely important as this is going to be the company that you will want to grow with and stay with for a long period of time. You want to make sure that the company you join feels like one that you are excited about and that you can happily stay with and support for a long period of time, thus ensuring that your business and your residual income has the longevity that you need to succeed.

Chapter 3: Committing to the Idea

Joining a network marketing company is a big decision for most people, and it can come with a lot of stressors and difficulties early on, especially if you are surrounded by people who are not particularly supportive of network marketing companies. It is important that once you decide to join a network marketing company, you commit to the idea and go completely all in on building your company and growing your network. There will likely be people and experiences along the way that leads to you feeling unsupported or like you cannot grow your business, so you will need to be ready to stay committed to the idea even if you start experiencing a lack of support from those in your network. It is important that you realize that this lack of support is common, and most people who have advanced to high ranking positions within their company have experienced some degree of discomfort when sharing their businesses with their network at first. It is not uncommon for people to accuse new network marketers of being duped by a scam or dragged into an annoying system, and then attempt to shame or humiliate the person for doing so. Unfortunately, this will happen at times and you will need to be ready to understand that not everyone will support you and then be prepared to stay committed to your success anyway. In this chapter, you are going to learn about how you can commit to your decision and stand behind your choice to join a network marketing company and grow with that company so that you can start earning the income that you intended to earn when you first chose to join the company.

Taking Responsibility for Your Success

The first thing that you need to do when it comes to joining a network marketing company is to take responsibility for your own success. A common mistake that new network marketers make is joining a company and expecting that success will be handed to them either by their upline showing them exactly what to do and handing them success or by their existing network buying into their business right away. The reality is that the only person who can help you generate success is yourself, and you need to be willing to put in the effort to generate your success from day one. If you rely on your upline to lay out the path to success for you or your existing market to be willing to buy your products and maintain your business, you are going to be leaving a lot of money on the table. You may also find yourself engaging in toxic marketing behaviors that alienate you from your friends and family and leave you struggling to generate any success, possibly to the point that you even become resentful of your business.

It is imperative that from day one, you look at your network marketing company as a business and you treat it like it truly is a business of your own. You need to be willing to do what it takes to reach out to people and gain the guidance that you need, to educate yourself on how marketing works, and to learn how to effectively handle and close sales calls. A lot of the information that exists out there is rather outdated or ineffective, so it is important that you do your part by reading books just like this one that will educate you on topics like attraction marketing or positive marketing strategies so that you can effectively reach your warm market.

You should start taking responsibility for your own success before you ever even sign up for a company by making the commitment to look at your business as your own business and treat it as such. Be prepared to be hands-on with tasks like generating your schedule, reaching out to leads, following up with potential customers, and educating your audience on the products and promotions that you have available. Consider everything that a business does, from marketing and working with customers to taking payments and filing taxes, be ready to do all of that. If you are not entirely familiar with what it takes to run a business, you might start following some successful network marketers and learn about how they do it or following other business owners in general and gaining tips from them. The more you educate yourself and implement the practices of successful business people early on, the better your understanding of marketing and business ownership will be which means that you will be directly setting yourself up for success.

Learning to Make Your Own Opportunities

As a business owner, you need to understand that it is not your clients' responsibility to make opportunities for you but it is your responsibility to make opportunities for yourself. While marketing and sharing in your social network is a great opportunity to start connecting with more potential leads and earning sales in your business, there are also many other ways that you can start generating opportunities for yourself. Exactly what methods you use will depend on what your company offers, who you serve, and where those people can be found. That being said, the number one thing that you can do to help you begin building your business and creating opportunities for yourself is to learn how to network and market in an organic manner through active, friendly conversations.

Many people put a lot of pressure on how to build their network and how to transition from a friendly conversation into talking about the business that they are in. The reality of the matter is, the conversation will only be as awkward or as uncomfortable as you make it, so the more confident you feel in leading the conversation, the more effective you will be in generating leads through your network. At first, it may feel uncomfortable or you may feel strange marketing your new business, especially if you are surrounded by people who generally frown upon network marketing or who believe that it is a scam. As you continue to talk about it and show that you are determined to be one of the ones at the top and that you are not being a pressure-based sales consultant, your audience will relax around you and warm up to the idea of your business. The process of your audience relaxing will also allow you to relax and feel more confident in sharing your business, thus enabling you to be more effective in sharing your company with people.

In addition to continually practicing your sales conversations and talking about your opportunity to those in your network, you need to be regularly building your network and meeting new people. Eventually, your existing network will be tapped out and you will want to connect with even more potential customers or recruits in order to continue growing your business even further. You can do this by starting conversations just about anywhere you go, which will enable you to gradually meet more and more people. If you want to have a bigger impact, however, attending larger events and connecting with more people this way is a powerful way to start growing your network more rapidly so that you can create even more opportunities for yourself. If your goal is to start expanding your network to support your business specifically, make sure that you are doing so by spending time at events that are actually relevant to your niche and that will likely be filled with people from your audience. The easiest way to do this is to think about who your target audience is, what events they are likely to attend, and which events are going to offer you the best opportunity to actually communicate with and talk to those individuals. So, choosing to attend networking events, charity gatherings, and other similar social events will offer you greater opportunities compared to choosing quiet events like the opera or theatre events where socializing is typically limited.

Seeking Help from Your Upline

The intimidation of not knowing what to do, or how to do it, can lead to anyone feeling as though they are unable to succeed with an opportunity that they have been offered. When it comes to network marketing, this is no different as you are entering a career that requires skills that you may not yet know how to use. Instead of launching your business and then existing in a perpetual state of overwhelm where it feels as though you will never be able to generate success because there is so much that you do not know about, reach out to your upline and request support. Ask for them to guide you, train you, and point you in the direction of valuable training materials so that you can educate yourself on how your business works, how to effectively market your products, and what you can do to bring more clients and consultants into your business. As you listen to your upline, make sure that you pay attention and validate what they are saying against what is currently accurate in marketing. A common mistake that new consultants make is assuming that the exact same marketing strategies that worked for their upline will work for them, which unfortunately leads to outdated marketing strategies being shared amongst the network marketing community. What you need to remember is that your upline already has a massive team, and at this point, it does not matter if they are actively marketing effectively because there are so many people beneath them in their network tree that are helping them continually grow their business.

What you need to be looking for from your upline is information regarding how to stay devoted, how to stay positive, and how to stay consistent. Pay close attention to the marketers who are making other opportunities for themselves as well, as these are the individuals who are taking the time to educate themselves on relevant marketing trends so that they can provide you with great information as well. It is important that you pay close attention to your upline specifically, as they are the ones who are going to have the information that is relevant to both marketing in general and marketing with your specific company, so they will have the best information as to what will work.

It is important that you vet every upline that you listen to, as not all upline members are created the same and you only want to learn from those who have the right information to support you. Avoid listening to anyone who is using outdated strategies, who is not actively recruiting new members themselves, or who is not generating a consistently high amount of income in their own businesses. You can conclude that by their present success or reputation that these individuals are not educated in what it actually takes to generate success in your business, thus meaning that the information you gain may not be valuable in supporting your growth.

Learning from Industry Leaders

Finally, in addition to listening to your upline, directly listen to other industry leaders who are generating massive success in network marketing. Even though not all of these individuals will be coming from your own business, they will have a significant understanding of what it takes to generate success in network marketing, what challenges you are likely to face, and what you can do to overcome those challenges in your life. Pay close attention to these individuals, follow them, and if they offer any, take their training courses so that you can learn more about how they generated their own success and how you may be able to apply their techniques to your own success. The more you surround yourself with people who are generating success, the easier it is going to be for you to stay inspired and positive about your ability to succeed, motivated in achieving your goals, and educated on what the industry is evolving into.

In addition to following industry leaders in network marketing specifically, follow industry leaders that are relevant to the niche that you are actively selling in. So, if you are selling health supplements, pay attention to individuals who are considered industry leaders in the health and wellness industry as these individuals are going to help educate you on what is going on in the health and wellness world. Paying attention to not only what is going on in the network marketing industry but also what is going on in the niche that you are marketing in will support you in marketing in alignment with your niche and staying on trend and relevant. You can also learn interesting and valuable marketing strategies from other industry leaders in your niche, even if they are not network marketers, that will support you in generating new ways to share your products and opportunity with people from your target audience.

The more you surround yourself with people who know what they are doing and who have generated the type of success that you desire to generate, the easier it will be for you to grow in your industry. Once again, if you are new to network marketing or if you have never generated success with a network marketing company before, you can guarantee that you are not yet educated on the skills that are required to help you generate success with your opportunity. Following leaders and individuals who are already generating success will help you stay focused on what you need to be doing in order to get to where you desire to go. Avoid spending time with anyone who bashes your industry, either from a network marketing perspective or a niche-specific perspective, as these individuals will only lead to you feeling defeated and struggling to grow forward. Surround yourself with empowering idols who can support you instead, as these are the individuals who are going to help you get to where you want to go.

Chapter 4: Finding Prospects

Finding prospects for your network marketing business is important, as this is how you are going to be able to find people who want to purchase your products or join your team. A big part of your marketing business is going to be constantly aligning yourself with new prospects who are going to be interested in joining your team or trying your products so that you can grow your business. To put it simply, the more people who buy from you or join you, the more you are going to make money. Since you are likely in network marketing to make a lot of money, you will need to emphasize on your goal of meeting plenty of new people and bringing them into your business opportunity. Of course, as your team begins to grow, you will find that you no longer need to do quite so much work yourself because your downline will also support you in growing your team, but even then, you would still want to continue growing your own prospect list. The more you grow, and the more that those in your downline grow, the more money you will all make.

In this chapter, you are going to learn about how you can promote your products and find new prospects who are interested in learning more about your company. The strategies in this chapter are important to pay attention to, as they all work together to leverage a strategy known as "attraction marketing" which is the new future of marketing in general. Many of the outdated network marketing strategy books will support you in using outdated marketing practices that result in you coming off as being annoying, spammy, or even a scam artist to your audience. While they may have worked in the past, they certainly do not work in today's world where people want to be attracted to the business they are looking to purchase from or join rather than pushed or convinced into it by someone in their network.

Always Be on the Lookout

The first thing that you need to do is to learn how to always be on the lookout for new prospects who may be interested in learning more about your brand. In the past, this would mean talking to everyone and presenting everyone with your opportunity so that everyone had the chance to hear you out and potentially join your team. These days, it has been proven that this strategy is no longer effective and that the better way is to start identifying who your ideal team members or customers are and only presenting your opportunity to these individuals so that you are not coming off as annoying or pushy to anyone else. In order to do this, you want to make sure that you are very clear on who your target audience is and how you can effectively identify them both online and offline. The clearer you are on how you can identify your target audience, the easier it will be for you to know when you are actively in a conversation with someone who may like to hear more about the opportunity that you have. As well, the easier it will be for you to find actual groups of your target audience and tap into these groups so that you can open yourself up to many prospects in one go.

In your day to day life, do not be afraid to keep your eyes peeled for areas where your prospect clients or consultants are hanging out and then do what you can to position yourself in front of these individuals. If you strike up a conversation with someone new who seems like they would be a good fit, for example, do not be afraid to consider them as a potential prospect and offer your opportunity to them. If you are planning on joining a new class or heading to an event, do not be afraid to identify whether or not your target audience will be there, and if they are, do not be afraid to start networking with them so that you can generate new leads.

When you are always on the lookout for prospects, you can ensure that you are ready and willing to position yourself in front of them so that you can open up your opportunity to a new person. Remember, you are not going to want to go out of your way and be pushy to talk to these individuals about your opportunity and draw them in. Instead, you would be better off to introduce yourself, generate a relationship with these people first, and then present your opportunity later on. So, instead of telling everyone and their Grandma that you have a new opportunity that they may be interested in, build a relationship and allow it to come up in an organic conversation some time in your relationship. You can always intentionally bring it up within the first few times that you meet with this new person, but do not go out of your way to pressure it into your first conversation with the individual as this will only come off as pushy. In modern times, if you try too hard to talk about what you do with network marketing, people may develop a fear around you potentially being another person who will push your opportunity on them. You need to make sure that your prospects see you as different, confident, and empowering so that when they learn about your opportunity, they do not feel like the only reason you are talking to them is to attempt to make a sale.

Use Success Stories to Sell

One of the best ways to sell your products in network marketing is through success stories, which show your audience just how powerful the products or services you are using actually are and what they can do for people. It is important that when you share success stories, you are sharing them in a way that actually gains people's interests and has them paying attention to what you are doing, as this is a great access point when it comes to attraction marketing. Physically showing someone the before and after snapshots of someone's success with your company is a chance to directly show people that your opportunity is real, that it works, and that it has changed lives. One of the biggest reasons why people will be hesitant around network marketing products is because naysayers have been very effective at asserting that no network marketing company offers high-quality products that actually work. Of course, the people who join network marketing companies and use their products know that this is not true, and you need to make sure that you show your audience it is not true, either.

If you are already friends with people in the network marketing industry and you scroll through your timeline on almost any platform, you are likely to see a lot of generic before and after pictures with the same people and the same stories being shared from multiple consultants.

This type of behavior can show that your products work, but it can also show people that you may not have enough positive testimonials for each of you to offer unique stories on who your products have worked for. That is why, if you want to generate success in attracting new prospects through this strategy, you need to start accumulating your own testimonials. Instead of relying on the ones that your upline offers for you to share with your audience, start using the products yourself and sharing them as a testimonial for what the results of using your products are. You can also start getting your friends and family using the products so that they, too, can start seeing results and can offer you positive testimonials regarding the products or services that you are offering. The more that you can create and accumulate your own personal testimonials from people that you know, the more personal your stories will be and therefore the more interested others are going to be in your stories. People grow more interested primarily because the individuals who are seeing positive results are people they are likely to know or people that you know personally so they can trust that these testimonials are genuine and authentic, rather than generic or potentially crafted. This level of trust and personal involvement result in people generating a far higher interest in your products than they would likely have if you had no connection to the people who are gaining results from your products.

In addition to getting your own personal network using the products and generating results, pay attention to other consultants in your company who have had massive or miraculous results from the products that you are selling. If someone in your upline, for example, lost a great deal of weight on your company's weight loss program, pay attention to them and listen to what their main points were, before they lost weight and how they feel now that they have. Use their testimony as an opportunity to generate new content for your audience so that you can highlight the struggles they may be facing now and offer them with a real insight as to what their life could look like if they used your products or services. In addition to using their stories to support your growth, you also want to get yourself directly around these individuals so that you can take pictures with them and establish a visual connection with them for your followers. That way, when you talk about how inspired you are by your upline, your personal audience and potential prospects see that your upline is a real person and that you have personally met them and gotten to know their story. When you establish personal connections like this, people tend to trust the stories that you are sharing in a more intimate way and they are more likely to want to pay attention to what you are sharing with them.

Leveraging Social Media and Email

Social media and emails are two of the most powerful marketing tools that we have in our current generation as they allow network marketers to market beyond their personal social circle and into a global market. When you are building your network marketing company, it is imperative that you get on social media and start growing your email list so that you have far more people to market to, thus allowing you to grow your network larger and faster. Using social media and email to market your network marketing business is going to prove to be a goldmine for your growth, but only if you leverage these two digital marketing platforms effectively. It is important that you educate yourself on the etiquette of how to use these platforms so that when you start marketing your company on them, you come across as authentic, genuine, and interesting. Abuse of these platforms such as overuse or treating them like online advertising facilities can result in you getting blocked, ignored, or even treated rather poorly from those who you market to. In the network marketing industry, many people have not been taught how to properly use social media and email to market so that they are attracting prospects, rather than driving them away. Fortunately, this does not mean that digital marketing is saturated or that you cannot pave the way for your own success on these platforms, you absolutely can. The key here is to immediately set yourself apart from other network marketers and prove that you are authentic, genuine, and compassionate.

The two biggest things that you need to avoid with digital marketing is sending unsolicited messages and plastering your feeds with generic corporate made images of the products and services that you are offering. If you start cold messaging people with your opportunity, copying and pasting status updates about your company, or using the same pictures that everyone else is using, no one is going to pay attention to you because they have already seen and heard it all before. As a result, you will heavily struggle to tap into your target audience and gain their attention, which means that your business will never effectively take off.

What you need to do on social media and in your email marketing is brand yourself and bring your company into your personal brand. Start making a reputation for yourself as an individual by sharing the things that matter to you and that you are passionate about, and then bring your network marketing company into that image by showing how it supports you in living a better life. Share what you are passionate about and how your products fuel your passion or support your passion, and share what you are dreaming of and then talk about how your products fulfill your dreams. Make sure that when people see your profile, they think of you and how influential and inspiring you are so that people are likely to pay attention to you and feel inspired to try out your products.

As a part of growing your personal brand, make sure that every time you talk about your company and your products, you are doing so in a way that personalizes the information that you are sharing. Make your own graphics, share your own stories, write your own content, and make sure that everything you are talking about is unique to you. The more you personalize your marketing approach this way, the more people are going to recognize that you are not "one of the many" that is trying to recruit them or sell to them to increase their own numbers, but that you are your own person doing your own thing. People like to see individuals doing their own thing, as this is far more attractive and interesting since they have not yet seen who you are, how you share, or what is important to you. You stand out because you are different, and you can leverage your uniqueness to support you in growing your business and recruiting far more people than you ever would if you tried to do it the same way that everyone else is doing it.

Chances are, if you look at the most successful people in your upline, you will recognize that even if it is clear that their entire brand revolves around the company and its products, they are still sharing it in their own unique way. Rather than doing what the herd is doing, they are sharing their own stories, their own thoughts, and their own opinions on both life and the products so that people can get to know *them* and why *they* are so passionate about what they are sharing. That is exactly why they have generated so much success in their own businesses, and that is exactly what you need to do in order to generate so much success in your own as well.

Gauging Your Audience

When it comes to network marketing, you need to be able to gauge your audience or determine just how interested they are in the products that you have to share with them. One of the fastest ways to grow your business is to make sure that you are talking to people who care and who are interested in actually hearing about what you have to say so that when you are marketing, you are sharing with people who are likely to listen and pay attention. You can gauge your audience's level of interest based on how often they are interacting with your posts, what type of comments they are making, and how engaged they are in active conversations if your company comes up during a personal conversation. It is important that you are always paying attention to your audience's reactions so that you can ensure that you are talking to the right people and warming up your audience so that you can have more warm and hot leads ready to join you.

When it comes to gauging your audience, there are two things you need to be paying attention to — your overall audience's level of engagement and each individual person's level of engagement when you are talking to them. With your audience, you need to make sure that they are regularly showing interest in the content that you are sharing and that the people showing interest are actually members of your target audience or people who are likely to purchase your products. If you find that you are not gaining any traction with your audience, you will need to spend time understanding what about your strategy may be struggling to attract their interest and have them paying attention to what you are sharing. You may find that you simply do not have the right people in your network yet, that you are speaking in a way that comes off as a pushy or faux pas, or that you are not using the right language to attract them. Alternatively, it may be because you are not spending enough time engaging with these individuals and developing your relationship with them to be able to actually gain their interest. If you are marketing to people who do not personally know you enough to trust you or care about your opinion, chances are they are going to ignore you because they do not feel compelled to listen. This is why personal branding matters so much. This is an opportunity to let people get to know you and feel like a personal part of your life so that they are interested in exactly what you are sharing.

If you are in a personal conversation with someone and you start to see signs that they do not care about what you are talking about, such as their answers growing shorter or a continuous change in conversational direction, it is important that you respect this and stop talking about your business. Continually talking about something people do not want to talk about only leads in one of two directions: either they stop talking to you because they are bored of what you are talking about, or they become downright resentful and grow extremely frustrated with you and your business. If someone becomes bored, they will likely end the conversation and may be reluctant to start new conversations with you for fear of having another boring conversation that they do not want to be a part of. If they become angry, they may avoid you completely or even block you on social media to avoid having to see your content anymore because they have grown to be so annoyed by you not respecting that they were not interested. Both of these experiences are unwanted, as they lead to an unnecessary disconnection between you and someone else, which can be upsetting for both of you especially if you had already developed a relationship beforehand.

If you start talking to someone and they seem disinterested, stop talking about your opportunity and start focusing on building a relationship with them instead as this will show them that you have more to offer than just your business opportunity. This way, you establish a new friendship and you are able to continue developing that friendship over time. This person may then show interest later, or they may introduce you to more people in their own network who might be interested in the opportunity that you have available for them. When you are respectful of people and their interests and boundaries, you ensure that you are developing a positive reputation for yourself and your brand, which can help support you in further growth. Remember, as soon as you sign up with a network marketing company, you become a business professional and you need to handle yourself like a professional to ensure that you are building a positive reputation for yourself and your business. If you start handling situations with a lack of professionalism, consideration, and politeness, you can burn a lot of bridges and it can set you up for failure early on.

Chapter 5: Presenting to Prospects

As you start developing your business and marketing yourself and your opportunity to people, you are going to start generating prospects who are interested in learning more about the offers that you have available. The individuals who you want to start presenting to are individuals who have shown interest in learning more, whether that is through reaching out to you or through expressing interest in a conversation where you have had the opportunity to bring the topic up yourself. When you have received the interest from someone that suggests they want to learn more, it is time for you to start presenting your opportunity to prospects so that you can sell your products or recruit people to your team! Knowing how to present your opportunity is important, as the way that you handle yourself during this presentation is going to significantly impact the way people see you and perceive your business. It is important that you handle these conversations properly to ensure that people are seeing you and your opportunity as positive and worth paying attention to.

In this chapter, we are going to discuss how you can start presenting your opportunity to people and successfully closing sales in your network marketing business. It is important that you realize that presenting does take practice and time, so the first few conversations that you have may be awkward or uncomfortable and they may not go exactly as planned. This is all a part of the process of learning, and it is no different from training to develop new skills in any other business, so give yourself the opportunity to make mistakes and learn along the way. The more you present your opportunity to people, the more comfortable it will become and the easier it will feel for you to share what you have to offer. As a result of using the right skills and developing them effectively, you will be able to grow your business far faster, so make sure that you commit to the learning process.

Selling from Small to Large

When it comes to growing your network marketing business, there are going to be many different sizes of sales that you are presented with. You will have some people who just want to buy tester sized products, and you will have others who want to buy a full kit or join your business. As a commission-based marketer, it is obvious that the sales that are larger and come with a potential sign up will feel as though they come with significantly more pressure than the smaller ones, particularly because there is more money at stake here. That being said, the way that you go about selling to both smaller and larger clients need to be exactly the same to ensure that you are always closing your deals and paving the way for more positive connections in the future.

The number one thing that you need to understand when you are generating sales in your business is that the clients who shop with you or the consultants who sign up with you are all coming to you because you offer them a unique experience that they enjoy. The more you can personalize this experience and make it positive and enjoyable, the more people are going to want to do business with you, so you will need to focus on offering the same high-quality experience to each and every single person. Treat every person like they are your million dollar sale by being polite and professional, offering the support that they need, sharing all of the information that they request, and doing any extras that you can to make it a positive and enjoyable experience. The more you offer this high quality, luxurious service, the more people are going to enjoy doing business with you. If you have a low stake sale that will only sell one product, you need to treat them like a million dollar sale so that if they love that product, they will come back and purchase more or join, and if you have a high stake sale, you treat them the same way so that they feel confident and empowered in their decision.

You can create high-quality sales by being available to serve the people that you are selling to. Pay attention to their needs, listen to their wants, and offer the best solutions based on what they care about and what they are looking for. Let the selling process be a part of your relationship building process, as you show them that you are there as a professional to support them in having an exceptional experience through your business. If you can, put together their cart for them, offer to take their payment information, and process the order for them so that all they need to do is share what they are interested in and you take care of the rest. If you can afford to, throw in a bonus or some samples with their order to make it extra special, or have it ship to you first so that you can include a personalized thank you note in the order. These types of special bonuses make shopping with your company a special and enjoyable experience that leads to people wanting to shop with you again. This experience also creates a positive foundation for anyone who desires to join you, as it shows them that they are going to be led by someone who knows exactly what they are doing and who can provide them with the best support in building a successful business.

Accepting the Word "No"

When it comes to sales, it is important that you learn how to accept the word "no" and stop upon hearing it. In any industry, one of the most frustrating things we can experience is someone not respecting that we are not interested in purchasing from them at this time, and it can lead to a tarnished reputation for the individual or company that is not respecting our boundaries. If you want to generate a positive reputation for yourself in your industry and start earning more sales and recruits in your business, respecting when someone says the word "no" and refraining from further pursuing them is extremely important. This type of respectful behavior can lead to individuals continuing to respect you and appreciate you even after they have determined that they are not currently interested in the offer that you have presented them with. When you behave this way, people begin to see that you are different from others and that you will respect their boundaries when you set them, which means that they are more likely to continue paying attention to you and your marketing posts even after this rejection.

As a network marketer, it is important that you value and respect every person in your network, even if they are not going to become your customers or recruits as these individuals may just introduce you to your next top-selling recruit. Furthermore, by respecting their "no" right now, you may find that they will come back later and choose to join with you or purchase products from you when the time suits them better. Sometimes, sales presentations can begin at a time where someone is not yet ready to hear what you have to offer, or they are not yet in a position to be able to join you. The person that you are pitching to may have just experienced a bad day or felt frustrated at the moment, or they may have not yet had the money to invest and so they say no for the time being. In this situation, being respectful and honoring their boundaries ensures that when they are in a position to listen, buy, or join your company, they are still readily willing to pay attention when the timing is better.

After someone has said no to you, the best protocol is to respect it and then leave the conversation alone until they approach you again. When you attempt to continually approach someone who has already said no, you show that you do not respect their boundaries and it leaves them feeling frustrated and annoyed with you. Then, rather than introducing you to their network or considering your offer in the future when the timing suits them better, they ignore you or eliminate you from their network altogether, which means that you have officially burned a bridge. This type of behavior will significantly slow down your growth rates or destroy your credibility and lead to your overall failure faster than any other strategy out there, so always show respect and courtesy for those who have said no to you.

Upselling Your Clients

If you are in the process of selling to someone and they are showing interest in products that you have available, upselling is a great opportunity to have them put through a bigger order, or even choose to join rather than simply purchase for all of the additional perks they gain. When it comes to network marketing, knowing how to upsell clients is a great opportunity to ensure that you are maximizing your income every single time. Upselling is a great strategy, but it follows all of the same rules as typical sales. Use this as an opportunity to further establish your relationship with the person and to personalize their experience even more, and if they say no, respect their no.

Most network marketing companies are structured in a way that offers an incredible opportunity to upsell your clients to bigger packages, which makes this part of the process a lot easier. That being said, it would be valuable for you to educate yourself on what the packages are in your business and understand how they work, including what products are involved and what the savings is like, to ensure that you feel confident in sharing these offers with your audience. The more you understand what your products are, how the product systems work, and what your clients' investment each package is, the easier it is for you to talk about these offers and upsell them.

If you have a client that is interested in your products and seems to express interest in the idea of network marketing, this is a great opportunity to upsell them to a consultant package. When you do, make sure that you are open and honest about what becoming a consultant entails and how it may benefit them, or how your client may be able to turn the opportunity into a profitable business venture for themselves. Make sure that as you share, you highlight the benefits that you think would appeal most to the client who you are selling to so that you can ensure that they are hearing only what truly matters to them. As you do this, do not hold back any information or change the truth to make the offer sound more suited to their needs, but instead make sure that you are clarifying how you think they may be able to work it into their lives and why you think becoming a consultant would benefit them. When people can see how and why network marketing would fit into their lifestyle, they tend to feel more open to the idea of joining and becoming a consultant under you so that they, too, can benefit from the values of being a consultant of your business.

Closing Sales

The final part of ending a sales call or presentation is closing sales with your customers. How you close your sale is going to depend on where your customer is at in the sales process, meaning whether or not they have already mentally committed to purchasing something from your company. If they have, then your only job is to make sure that you put the products in front of them and direct your client through the checkout process. If you can, (like mentioned before) you might even consider taking their payment information or having them pay you directly and then you personally submit the order for them so that your client simply has to mention what they would like and you take care of everything else. Offering this full-service checkout experience can be quite luxurious, and it also ensures that the checkout process is simple and that the order is finalized.

If your client has not yet mentally committed to purchasing from you, you are going to need to spend some time paying attention to what may be holding them back from wanting to buy your products or services. In some cases, they may have missed the point where they saw how the products would benefit them personally, or they may have not felt as though your presentation completely touched down on their main points and offer a solution. If this is the case, you can easily get to the end of the sale by talking less and listening more so that you can genuinely pay attention to what your client needs and what they are looking for. Then, all you need to do is rephrase what they have said to you and offer them solutions that directly serve what they need so that they can feel confident in your products' ability to fulfill their needs.

It is important that you never consider a sale "closed" until the person has checked out and they have paid money for their products. Until a person has completely finalized a check out process, they have not yet completed their sale which means that they are not committed yet. If you are not paying attention, these sales can fall through as people may forget to check out or back out due to a number of different reasons that could easily be rectified had you paid attention and offered your support along the way. For example, maybe your client wanted to check out but read something on the website and misunderstood what it meant or felt like the checkout process was confusing and so they decided to put it off instead. If you were there to support them, the checkout process would be easier and they would have the option to ask you to clarify a piece of information for them to ensure that they feel confident in the products that they are ordering. Staying involved and remaining committed to being of service to your customers during the entire sales process, including the closing and even after the purchasing process is important as this is how you can show your customers that they genuinely matter to you. This shows positive business sense and that you are interested in building genuine relationships with your clients, and that you are not just another network marketer attempting to add them to your list of sales so that you can achieve your next bonus.

Chapter 6: The Follow-Up

One of the most important conversations that you will ever have with a person in your network is your follow up conversation, which allows you to keep yourself in the forefront of someone's mind, offer additional service if it is needed, and ensure your customers are completely satisfied. Many times, network marketers or businesses in general will leave money on the table and fail to maintain positive relationships with their customers because they simply do not invest enough energy into maintaining a positive follow up practice.

Following up with someone, whether they have already purchased with you or not, is your opportunity to make sure that they are satisfied and that they know that you are available to support them if need be. There are four times when you are going to need to follow up with someone: after pitching the products but before they have purchased, after they have purchased, after you have pitched your opportunity but before they have joined, and after they have joined your company. These are all vital times to follow up with someone as it allows you to support them in finalizing their decision if they have not already, or ensure that they are satisfied with their decision if they have already purchased or joined. Here, you can ensure that if there is anything extra that can be done to support them in having the best experience possible that you fulfill that right away and that their experience is outstanding. That way, you are more likely to have people come back as repeat clients, or commit even more to their businesses and grow underneath you, which results in your business growing even further.

In addition to being able to support people in having a better experience with you and your company, offering a follow up also allows you to keep your warm and hot markets active. When you are building a business, gaining repeat sales or helping someone who has already joined grow their business is easier than reaching out to new individuals who have not yet purchased or joined your company. Although you do regularly want to be bringing in new customers and consultants to grow your business, you also want to be nurturing your existing network so that they feel confident in doing business with you and that they continue purchasing from you. One of the biggest reasons why your existing network is so powerful is because they already know how awesome your products are and how easy it is to do business with you which means that they are more likely to want to purchase again and share their experience with their own network. As you continue to build your name and reputation with your existing audience, they begin to share it with their audience and direct more people into your network. As a result of this positive feedback and growth, even more people are drawn into your business and your growth continues. Furthermore, customers who regularly refer people to you to purchase products or who experience people showing interest in the products that they are using get to see how easy it would be if they were to market the products themselves, which means that they may be more likely to join! So, as often as you are working on building up your network and drawing more people into your sales opportunity, make sure that you are also nurturing your existing network and ensuring their satisfaction. The combination of these two practices will support you in experiencing a far greater amount of success in your network marketing career going forward.

Timing Your Follow Up

Everyone has their own network marketing strategy, so you will to need to generate your own along the way to make sure that you are maintaining a follow-up system that works best for you and your audience. It is important that you pick a system that feels natural for you as this will ensure that it feels natural for your audience, too, which helps them stay attracted to and interested in your business and the offers that you have available.

The first step in building your own strategy is timing your follow up to ensure that you are getting back to people after they have had enough time to think things through and before they have had enough time to talk themselves out of it or get distracted and lose interest.

Achieving this timing takes practice as you will need to identify how long it takes with your particular audience to feel as though they have had enough time to think things through. Typically, the companies that offer more expensive products or services or that offer something that has a greater impact on someone's life, such as insurance, will require slightly more time in the follow up as people will need to think things through. Companies with lower entry offers or less pressure around the products will tend to have an easier time closing sales relatively quickly, as the individuals purchasing will not need to consider their finances or emotionally digest what it is that they are seeking to purchase.

The best way to time your follow up is to simply ask what feels right for your client, as this gives them the chance to determine whether or not they feel like your follow up window offers them enough time to actually consider whether or not they are ready to invest. This works best if you are chatting with a client who is interested in purchasing or joining but has not yet taken the leap, thus leaving them feeling as though they need to think things through a little longer. You can easily say something like "Great, I know you said you want more time to think this through. Would it be okay if I followed up with you in three or four days?" This way, you can let your prospect determine whether or not that feels like enough time, and if they say okay, you know exactly when you need to get back in touch with them regarding the product or kit that they were most interested in. All you need to do then is to book the follow up in your calendar and message them back on the date that you agreed upon.

If you are following up with someone who has already purchased from you, whether it was a product or a consultant kit, you will want to give them some time to make sure that they feel as though they have had a chance to test things out and look around for themselves. Typically, following up one to two weeks after they have purchased or joined is a great amount of time to ensure that they have had a chance to experience the product or system and get a feel for it themselves. Then, all you need to do is ask if they are enjoying it and if there is any way that you can improve their experience or support them in feeling more satisfied. If they do suggest anything, you can easily offer a solution for them to support them in feeling more confident, and if they do not, you can thank them for their time and their purchase and offer to support them when they need assistance in the future.

In addition to following up with someone who has already purchased products to ensure that they are satisfied, you will also want to follow up with them shortly after to see if they are ready to refill their products yet. It is extremely easy for people to think about getting a refill but then forget about it or simply not go through with purchasing one because it always seems to be too much hassle at the point when they remember. Even though shopping is usually quite simple, not everyone will feel like going through the process of adding products to their cart and paying for the contents of their cart and waiting for the shipping information. This is why it is important that you follow up with them and offer to support them with purchasing more products when they are ready because they know that they can then rely on you to process the order for them and they simply pay you for the experience. In order to time these follow-ups, you will need to determine approximately how long it will take for someone to completely use up the products that they have received and need more. Ideally, you want to get back in touch with them long enough before the product runs out to ensure that they are not running out of products before they need more. Then, you can process the order for them early enough to ensure that they have more on the way so that they can seamlessly jump into using a new bottle or container of whatever you may be selling them!

If your company has an auto shipment process and your client has signed up for an auto ship, it is still important that you follow up with your clients before their auto shipment is due to processing. This is a great opportunity for you to remind them that the shipment is about to process, to ask if there is any way that you can improve their experience, and to ensure that they still want to get everything that is on the order. If they want to make any adjustments, you can offer to support them in changing their orders to ensure that they are not getting products that they may not want or need. Since one of the biggest selling points of an auto ship for many companies is being able to change your monthly order while still maintaining the high-quality discounts on the products, it is important that you remind your customers to change their orders if this is what they aim to do. This is a simple way to make sure that your customer always feels supported and like they are gaining the best service possible, ensuring that they are more likely to continue ordering through you and using the products that they are shipped.

Organizing Your Follow-Up System

Organizing your follow up system is essential as it ensures that you are not going to miss out on any important follow-up experiences. There are two ways that you can organize your follow up system: digitally or manually, depending on what feels best for you. If you are frequently on your phone and if you find the calendar on it to be easy to use, using the calendar directly in your phone to schedule your follow-ups is a great way to make sure that you are prepared to follow up with every single person as needed. Alternatively, you can always keep a planner or a calendar nearby and jot down all of your follow up notes in there so that you know exactly what days you need to follow up with what people. If you do it this way, make sure that you read through the book every single day so that you are aware of who you need to connect with on each day.

In addition to storing information about who needs to be followed up with and when, it can also be valuable to write down important notes about the person that you are following up with. For example, you can write down information such as what they were interested in, what they needed to think about or what needed to happen before they could decide, and what products or packages you think would best fulfill their needs. This way, when you begin the follow up process, you already know exactly what you need to know in order to be able to follow up and share information that is actually relevant to what your prospect is looking for, rather than following up and needing to start fresh or requesting information that they have already shared to you before. Being able to personalize the follow-up experience is a great opportunity to ensure that you are showing how much you care about the person that you are following up with and how committed you are in helping them have a positive experience. When you go the extra mile, people tend to notice it and they are far more likely to reciprocate that energy by going the extra mile with you, too, such as through purchasing more products or joining your team.

Effective Follow-Up Strategies

The follow-up strategies that you use need to be effective to ensure that when you are reaching out to follow up with people, you are actually gaining traction with the process. You want to make sure that you are following up in a way that feels organic and friendly and not pressured or overwhelming. You also want to make sure that you are doing it in a way that honors the other person's space and does not make it feel like you are crowding in on them or trying to push them into a sale, as these types of behaviors can significantly slow down your success rates. Furthermore, a poor follow up system can also result in your prospect feeling put off by you or your business which can lead to you losing a prospect rather than gaining a sale or a recruit.

There are two ways that you can arrange for follow-ups to happen: automatically or manually. The best automatic system to use in network marketing is an email newsletter which enables you to send emails to individuals periodically throughout the month to let them know of your upcoming sales or the offers that you have available. These newsletters can also spotlight products, give tips and ideas on how your customers can use the products in their daily life, and share other valuable information with them that may be relevant to your niche or your business. When you share these emails, make sure that they offer plenty of valuable content that encourages people to feel excited to open them and read the information inside. The more people open these emails, the more they are going to see the marketing that is inside of them as well which makes them more likely to actually pay attention to your products and services. If your email just looks like a coupon or a catalog page, chances are they will begin to ignore the messages that you send because it feels like you are simply trying to gain more sales.

When you are adding people to your email newsletter, make sure that you request their permission, first. Many places require people to have consent for individuals to join a newsletter, otherwise it is considered to be spam and can be grounds for legal action. You can easily request someone's permission by simply asking them if they would be interested in joining your newsletter so that they can receive great information about the products and services that you offer. Let them know that the newsletter is packed with valuable content and that it will support them in achieving their desired goals or making the most out of their new products so that they can see why it would be a good idea for them to join your email list. If they say no, make sure that you do not add them to your email list as this is a violation of their privacy and can lead to you losing credibility in your business and being seen as disrespectful and spammy.

Manually following up with people is best done at the four points mentioned above: before they have committed to either purchase or join, or after they have purchased or joined. Following up with people manually means that you message them, email them, or call them directly to ask them how their experience has been so far and if you can be of service in supporting them any further. Your entire follow up call should be devoted to being of service to the person that you are following up with to ensure that they trust that you will be available to support them if they need it, even if they do not actively need the support right in that minute.

When you manually follow up with people, make sure that you do it in the way that best suits that individual so that you are respecting their desires. You can figure that out by asking them what feels best or by reaching out to them in the same way that you conducted your sales call as you know that this is their most comfortable point of connection. By connecting with people in a way that feels comfortable to them, you make sure that their entire experience is positive and that they feel that they can reach out to you for support anytime that they need it. Keeping this line of communication open and relevant is going to be powerful in helping you grow your business, which will ensure that you are able to increase your credibility and reputation and maximize your growth over time.

As you conduct the follow-up call or chat, make sure that you are friendly and relatable. Make the follow-up call conversational so that it feels easy for your customer to open up to you about any concerns that they may be having or easy for them to do business with you again. If you become too professional and keep the conversation stiff, your customer may feel as though you are reading from scripts or being inauthentic during the conversation which can reduce your credibility. The best balance when conducting a follow-up call is to remain professional and charismatic so that you can continue building your relationship with your customer or your new recruit.

Chapter 7: Promoting Products and Events

If you are a network marketer, make no mistake that the primary skill that you need to tap into with your company is learning to promote your products! When you are promoting products, you give people the opportunity to see the many reasons why you have joined your company, why you use these products on a regular basis, and why you are so passionate about them. Sharing your products also gives you the opportunity to let people know what you currently have to offer, what sales they can take advantage of, and how they can get the best savings while shopping for your products.

When it comes to network marketing, it is important that you promote effectively so that your products can reach the eyes of interested buyers and actually interest them. A reality that you are going to have to face is that many people have a poor concept of what it means to be a network marketer which can lead to people automatically tuning you out, so showing people that you are different and marketing authentically can help you increase your sales. In this chapter, you are going to learn how to promote your products in an effective way that allows people to see how incredible they are, to develop a positive relationship with you right from the very start, and to get your products in the hands of interested buyers. These strategies are the most up to date strategies for you to use starting right away, but it is important that you continue to pay attention to how marketing is evolving over time so that you can continue to market yourself in the most relevant and effective ways. The more you pay attention to current marketing trends and strategies, the easier it will be for you to continually grow your business to massive new heights.

Branding Yourself

Many people who enter network marketing believe that they have to brand themselves to their new company, but as you already know, it is more important that you build your product and company into your personal brand if you want to market effectively. The biggest reason why this matters is because when you are marketing, people want to know you and your story and they want to feel connected to what you are sharing. When you promote yourself and your life in a tasteful manner, people start following you because they are interested in what you have to share, which leads to them wanting to try out your products or join your team.

Personal branding alongside a network marketing company is fairly simple, you just need to showcase your lifestyle and talk about how your company and products fit into your life. This shows people that they do not need to completely change their way of living in order to use your products or join your team, which makes them feel as though it would be easier to get started and join you. As a result, they are more likely to reach out to you and pay attention to what you are doing, and they feel inspired to believe that they can easily do the same thing and start earning an income as well.

You can start promoting yourself in many ways, including sharing personal stories and anecdotes from your day to day life that highlights your lifestyle in a way that resonates with your audience. The stories you share do not have to directly relate to your company, as long as they highlight parts of your life that people in your target audience are likely to experience as well. For example, if you are selling an aromatherapy kit that helps people relax and you are a busy Mom who regularly feels stressed out, talking about your life as a Mom and other ways that you infuse your life with peace in addition to your aromatherapy practices is helpful. This shows that you are able to provide massive value to your audience, that you are relatable, and that you are not strictly attempting to get your audience to purchase products from you. When you make yourself a human with multiple aspects to your reality and many things to talk about that would relate to your target audience, people are more interested in following you because they feel as though they are building a relationship with you, personally. As a result of this relationship, they are also more likely to trust in you and purchase your products.

Video Marketing Strategies

Video marketing is one of the most popular marketing strategies to exist in today's world as it provides brands and companies with the opportunity to provide a personal face for people to look at and build a relationship with. Since you are building a personal brand, you want to make sure that you are regularly hopping on video calls so that you can start generating more personal connections with the network that you are building on social media. If you are nervous about video marketing, rest assured that it gets easier in time and that as you grow used to using this strategy, you will also learn how to become more creative with it and share in a more authentic way.

If you are particularly nervous, you can start by just doing videos in a private Facebook group that you create to share with your audience, or by doing a live video together with another consultant who you feel comfortable around that can help you. You can also start by doing short video clips on stories instead of on live videos until you start feeling more comfortable with people seeing you on camera and interacting with your video content. The more you warm up to being on the camera, the easier it is for you to share with your audience this way and the easier it will be for you to generate more meaningful connections with your digital audience that is unable to see you in person on a regular basis, or ever.

When you do live videos, make sure that you are doing them for different reasons all the time. While hopping on a live video to share your latest product haul or promotions is a great opportunity to share, you want to make sure that this is not the only reason that you are doing lives as people will grow bored and stop paying attention. The best way to leverage live videos is to come on for many different reasons, each of which should include sharing value such as educational information or entertainment through the live video feed. Doing it this way will ensure that your audience is never entirely sure of what you will be sharing, thus making them more likely to tune in and pay attention to what you are talking about on your live video.

Once you have made a live video, make sure that you share it with your group and business page or personal page, depending on where it was originally filmed. The more times your video gets shared out, the more viewers you stand to gain which means that you are more likely to get seen by your target audience and generate a larger network or more sales through each feed. When it comes to digital marketing, each piece of content should be made at the highest quality possible which means that you are going to want to share it out or get as many views as you can to ensure that each piece of content is making the biggest impact possible. This way, you do not feel as though you are constantly scrambling to make more content because your existing content is working harder for you.

Targeted Content Curation

When you are marketing on a digital platform, it is important that you use targeted content curation to ensure that your content is actually resonating with your target audience and generating a higher level of traction for you. In the marketing world, it is important to understand that if you are not very specific with who you are talking to, then you are not going to be talking to anyone since no one will truly know who your content is made for or if they are meant to pay attention to what you are sharing. Even if your company already has a niche market, such as supplements for health and wellness, it can benefit you to get even clearer and focus on serving one or two niches through your own content. You want to pick niches that are relevant to you and that you can easily serve, which means that you yourself should be considered a part of your target audience because this way, you can ensure that you are the right person to actually be targeting this niche.

If you have never targeted a niche audience before or if you have never needed to create content for a specific audience before, learning how to work with client avatars to build your business can be a valuable tool for supporting you in creating the right content. A client avatar is essentially an avatar or a character profile that you create that outlines who your ideal client is and what makes them so interested in shopping with you or joining your team. You want to create an in-depth client avatar that essentially resembles a real person so that you can consider this avatar and generate content that feels as though you are talking directly to them every single time, thus allowing you to generate relevant content. The easiest way to create a client avatar as a network marketer is to consider one or two of your closest friends or family members who would be most likely to gain value from your company and then behave as though they are your client avatars. Every time you make content to post online, act as though you are sharing that content directly with them and talk about the things that they would care about most, or that they would be most interested in reading about. This type of targeting ensures that you are very clear in what you need to talk about, what parts of your company you need to market, and what type of content you need to share in order to connect with your audience.

When you are creating content, the other thing that you will need to consider is what type of content or what medium of content your audience is the most likely to pay attention to. For example, is your audience paying closer attention to stories than posts, or live videos over pictures? Pay attention to what topics they like to read about, whether they prefer how-to guides or personal anecdotes, and what other mediums of content they are most interested in paying attention to. As a marketer, you want to be generating content that is clearly designed for your target audience, so you will need to make sure that you are always focusing on the platforms and types of content that are most relevant to your audience. You can easily find out what this is and where this is by generating content specifically for your target audience and testing out multiple areas on platforms like Facebook, Instagram, Pinterest, and YouTube so that you can see where you are getting the most traction. The types of content that get you the most feedback should be the ones that you continue creating more of, and you can let everything else go.

Attending the Right Events

In addition to attending networking events where you are exclusively going to mingle and expand your connection, you can also attend events where you can actually promote and share your products with your target audience.

These events, also known as vendor events, are typically designed in a way where you get to show up and share your products with your target audience by having a display set up and sharing products and pamphlets with your audience. When done the right way, these events can lead to you having the best opportunity to make plenty of money and prospects in one go. That being said, you need to make sure that you are attending the right events and using the right tools to help you actually generate interest and grow your prospective audience and client list.

The first step which is finding the right events is typically the hardest step. Even so, this is not as challenging as you might think, especially when you have done it once or twice and you have connected with hosts in your area. Typically, the easiest way to start connecting with vendor event hosts is to join local Facebook groups dedicated to this topic or to start connecting with other local vendors and paying attention to where the markets are going to be. Then, all you need to do is determine which markets are going to be the most productive for you in a sense that they will be targeted toward exactly who you want to connect with. You want to avoid attending events that are not going to have many of your target audience members there as this will result in a low turnout and you will struggle to generate any success with your business. Instead, pay attention to attending events that are more relevant to your target audience and that will provide you with a higher chance of generating a more positive turnout. In addition, make sure that the events you are looking at are in your price range as you will actually need to pay to attend these events. You will want to put together a budget for yourself that outlines both the cost of the event itself and the cost of the materials that you are going to need to use to host the event. Typically, this will include a table cloth, some samples and brochures, and anything else required for you to share your products and company with the people who will pass by your booth for the duration of the event.

The second step in attending events is actually going to the event, displaying your business, and talking to the people who are walking past your booth. For this part, all you need to do is make sure that your display looks attractive and informative so that people are more likely to stop and listen to what you have to share with them. Another way to bring people into your table is to offer free samples or product testers on the spot that they can try so that they can immediately see whether or not they like what you are offering. This type of display motivates people to stop and also encourages them to immediately find out whether or not they like your products, thus inspiring them to slow down and either provide you with their information or book an order right away that evening.

If you have never hosted an event before or if you are afraid that you might not know enough about your company to share it with all of your passerby's, you might consider inviting someone from your upline to attend your event with you and start sharing information about your company. This is a great way to get on-the-spot training from your upline for hosting events, sharing your products, and conducting presentations with prospective clients or consultants. Once you start feeling more confident in doing shows, you can choose whether you want to continue doing them with a partner or if you want to start doing them on your own.

Showing Products in Use

The most effective way of marketing your products is to become a product of them yourself! Use your products in as many different ways as you can, try out and commit to using as many different types of products that you carry as you can, and let people see what that looks like. Do not only focus on using the products and sharing testimonials, but also show the products in use so that people can see first-hand what it looks like to use your company's products.

There are many creative opportunities that you can use to show your products in use, both directly and indirectly when it comes to marketing for your company. You can become creative in your own right or use Pinterest or another similar picture sharing platform to get an idea for how other people are sharing your company's products and share in a similar manner. As you do, focus on searching for unique ways of sharing, not the same ways that everyone else is using, as this will ensure that your pictures stand out from the other consultants who are sharing similar products.

To help inspire your creativity, let's consider a face mask that you may be selling as an example. You could easily promote this face mask in countless ways online, all through using the face mask directly in your posts. You could post a video of you applying the face mask, talk about how valuable the face mask is and why it is so unique, and then show you washing it off and talk about how your skin feels and how much you enjoy the mask as one way of marketing it. Then, in another post on another day, you could share a picture of you sitting cozy with a cup of tea and a book or your favorite show on the TV while the mask sets on your face. In this post, you could talk about how important it is to relax at the end of each day and how valuable the face mask has been to your relaxing routine. Another time, you could show a picture of you wearing the mask while brushing your teeth and talk about how vital it is as a part of your skin care routine and the many benefits that people gain from using that mask. If you are meeting with prospects in person, you could offer to bring the face mask along if it is appropriate to the event and apply the face mask for them so that they can physically experience it in action. The more ways that you creatively share your face mask with people and the more highlights you manage to draw out to share with others, the easier it is for you to show people how incredible the product is and gain their interest in wanting to try it.

The reason why showing products in use works better than simply posting inanimate pictures of them is because it gives more depth to the products being shared. When people see something in action, it becomes easier for them to grow interested in it and start picturing how it might feel for them to use or experience the product for themselves. When you combine showing the product in use with describing it and making it a complete experience, people instantly become curious about whether or not they would like using your product so they are more likely to purchase it in order to try it out.

Chapter 8: Handling Rejection

Rejection happens in every single business since not everyone is going to be ready to or interested in purchasing the products that you have available for them. When you start marketing your products, you are inevitably going to come across instances of rejection where people are simply not interested in trying what you have to offer. Learning how to handle rejection properly is important as it will prevent moments of rejection from causing you to feel as though you are failing in your business for any reason. It will also ensure that you can navigate rejection in a way that allows you to maintain a credible appearance and a positive reputation, thus meaning that rejection does not equal a bridge burned.

In this chapter, you are going to discover what the difference between objection and rejection is, and how to handle both of these experiences in your business. This deeper understanding of what it means to experience someone who is objecting to the sales process versus someone who is rejecting it altogether will help you determine whether or not you should continue to pursue that individual. Naturally, if a person has an objection, you can continue sharing with them and showing them the value of your company so that they can feel inspired to keep paying attention and overcome the objection so that they can give your product or company a chance.

If the person has rejected your offer, it is important that you accept this rejection and step back to avoid overwhelming the person or tarnishing your own credibility and reputation for not respecting someone else's choices.

Understanding the Difference Between Objection and Rejection

The difference between objections and rejections is simple: an objection can be overcome and a rejection cannot be. An objection signals that someone is interested in your products or company but feels that they cannot yet purchase anything or doubts whether or not the product is for them. Objections often come through as an indirect decline of your offer that is attached to some form of reasoning. For example, "this sounds awesome, but I cannot afford it right now" or "this sounds amazing, but I'm not sure that it will offer me the results that I am looking for." When you hear an objection, you know that you need to start offering more information to support the individual in making their choice. If the objection is money, offering an inexpensive solution or discount, or offering to follow up with your prospect at a better time is a great opportunity to overcome this objection so that you can share your products with your prospect and close your sale. If your prospect is in doubt whether or not your product is right for them, taking the time to listen to their doubts and offering information that can help them feel more confident in their choice is a great way to support them in overcoming their objection. The easiest way to overcome objections is to listen to exactly what your customer is objecting and offer the right information to help them make their choice or feel more confident in deciding to purchase from you.

When you are countering objections, your goal is never to manipulate someone into buying or pressure them into choosing to purchase anyway. When you behave this way, you may close a sale but you also generate the reputation of being someone who does not genuinely care about what their audience wants or needs, which can lead to people avoiding you or deeply regretting their purchase and even resenting you. Your goal, instead, is to listen to what they are saying and offer more information so that your customer can feel empowered to make the decision that is the right decision for them.

Respecting When No Means No

Sometimes, you are going to encounter people who reject your offer or who, after objecting, decide that they are uninterested and turn into a rejection altogether. One of the biggest mistakes that you can make is attempting to continually push your products or services onto this individual in an attempt to change their mind or pressure them into believing otherwise. You need to respect that when someone has made a decision not to purchase from you or join your company, that their answer is no and give them the right to maintain their no. If you were to try and pressure them into changing their mind, all that will happen is you will tarnish your reputation and lead them into believing that you are not an honorable person to do business with. This understanding of you will only further reinforce their desire to avoid working with you as they do not want to be subjected to your pushiness or aggressive marketing strategies any longer. In some cases, they may even block you, unfriend you, or say rude things to you because they feel like you are not respecting their boundaries and honoring their right to say no.

When it comes to running your business, rejection is going to happen often and you need to understand that being rejected simply means that you were marketing to the wrong person. Even if you genuinely believe that their product is the right one for you, you are going to need to set your beliefs aside and respect that they have decided against it. When you stop putting so much pressure on trying to change people's minds, you open up the opportunity for you to start sharing more openly with the people who would be interested in your offer. As a result, they are more likely to maintain their respect toward you and your business and may even become a valuable asset to your network in the future.

Making Rejection Easier To Manage

When it does come down to handling rejection, knowing how to navigate it from a personal perspective can be helpful in supporting you with feeling more confident in going through the process. When you realize that rejection is natural and that it is not a negative reflection on you or your company, it becomes a lot easier for you to bounce back from rejection and continue sharing and marketing your offer to those who are interested in your products. This way, you can continue bravely growing your business even though you are fully aware that it is not for everyone.

Put it into Perspective

The first thing that you need to do when it comes to handling rejection is put it into perspective. Many people struggle with rejection because they fear that people not liking their business means that they are going to fail. The reality is, your business is not meant for everyone and if you are connecting with people who it is not meant for, you simply need to recreate your marketing strategy so that you can have a greater impact in reaching your clients. Think of it this way, if a pizza shop was to open up near your home, not everyone would stop in to purchase pizza from the shop. Some people may choose against it because they cannot afford it, others may already have a pizza shop they like going to and so they do not want to go elsewhere, some may not go in because the marketing does not appeal to them, and others still may choose against going into the shop because they simply do not like pizza. There are many reasons why people do not want to go to the pizza shop, but at the end of the day, these people not going into the shop would not matter as long as the pizza shop was effectively reaching the people that did want to go in and purchase pizza.

The same goes for your business, it does not matter how many people do not want to shop from you as long as you are consistently connecting with people who do want to shop with you and who will happily come back. If you are not reaching people who want to buy from you, you may need to change your approach to ensure that you are targeting your audience effectively and writing the type of content that they need to read about in order to book with you.

Detaching from the Outcome
Another thing that you can do when it comes to selling products so that you are

prepared to handle any rejection is to detach from the outcome before you even start talking to your prospects. If you assume every single person is going to purchase from you, your rejection will feel a lot more painful because it will feel like more is at stake and like you are missing out on many sales. If, however, you detach from the idea that every single person is going to buy from you and you trust that as long as you keep doing your job the people who *do* want to work with you will show up, it becomes a lot easier for you to handle any rejection that you may face. When you detach, not only will the rejection hurt less, but it will also allow you to feel more at ease with responding in a positive manner to anyone who rejects your business offer or products.

Asking for a Reason

If you receive a rejection and you feel like the person may be open to continue communicating with you, you might consider asking that individual if they can provide you with a reason as to why they are rejecting your offer. Although it can be painful to ask for and listen to the reason sometimes, hearing what has caused someone to decline your offer gives you the opportunity to make any necessary adjustments that you may need to make in order to refine your approach. If you receive feedback about your personal approach or how you have conducted the call, it is important that you are polite and show respect for what the person says and consider adjusting your approach going forward so that you can experience more positive feedback in the future. If the feedback is in regards to your products themselves or the offers themselves, make sure that you review your marketing strategy to ensure that you are targeting the right people. Sometimes, you may find yourself receiving a lot of rejections if you are targeting the wrong people and they realize that you do not have to offer what they were actually looking for in the first place.

Avoiding Emotional Attachment

When it comes to running your own business, feeling emotionally attached to the outcome can become a real and challenging issue to deal with. Many people who get started in network marketing are not educated on how to separate business from personal and it can lead to feeling as though you are personally being rejected or hurt by the experiences that you are having in your business. If you do not learn to emotionally detach from your business opportunities, making sales and handling challenges in your business is going to feel extremely difficult as you will be struggling to understand that not everything is reflective of you as an individual. You can detach emotionally by putting things into perspective and remembering that every single person's experience, opinion, and review of your business is their opinion of your business, not you personally. If you start to receive personal commentary, remember that this person is only reflecting on one aspect of you, not you as a person but you as a consultant. Handle the conversation respectfully and then avoid doing business with or talking to that person again to ensure that you are not being subjected to their unkind and unfair treatment of you.

Chapter 9: A Winning Mindset

In order to succeed in any business venture, you need to have a mindset that is going to support you in generating the success that you desire. Creating a winning mindset for you to be able to succeed with ultimately requires you to be willing to do the inner work, pay attention to how your thoughts are affecting your actions, and change your habits and behaviors to ensure your personal growth. In this chapter, you are going to learn about mindset practices that you can start using right away to begin building the mindset that you need in order to succeed with running your own business.

Self-Discipline

If you want to be successful with running your own business, you will need to learn how to master self-discipline so that you can begin holding yourself accountable and making the changes necessary to create the success that you desire. It can be challenging to remain disciplined enough to generate success, but if you are willing to commit to yourself and your personal growth, creating the success that you desire will become a lot more achievable. Not only will it make achieving the success that you desire more achievable, but self-discipline will also support you in achieving heights greater than you ever dreamed possible, which ensures that you are going to have the best possible outcome every single time.

When you make a commitment to doing something in your life, whether it be making a change, learning a new skill, or adapting to a new situation, self-discipline allows you to genuinely commit to that change and stay impeccable with your word. This type of discipline shows you that you are willing to do whatever it takes to succeed which keeps you willing to show up and serve every day, and it shows your audience that you are committed as well which leads to them trusting in you and taking you seriously.

When you choose to run your business, define what success means to you and outline what it will take for you to generate the success that you desire. Then, start working toward creating that success every single day and refuse to give up until you see the success that you desire. If you find yourself not progressing in the way that you hoped you would, be disciplined enough to look at your strategy and reframe your approach rather than giving up and assuming that there is no possible way forward. The more disciplined you are with yourself and your business, the easier it will be for you to keep showing up, growing in the way that you need to, and serving your clients in the best way possible so that you can generate greater success in your business.

Mental Toughness

In business, it can be extremely easy to get swept away with fear or uncertainty and give into the worrying thoughts that you have that lead you to feel like you simply cannot proceed. If you lack mental toughness, every negative review, rejection, stagnant phase, and challenge is going to set you off and leave you feeling like there is no possible way for you to proceed in running your business and succeeding. If you have mental toughness, however, succeeding becomes a lot easier because you trust that you will have what it takes to create the outcome that you desire. You will be able to reframe and heal from harsh words or cruel opinions, stay focused and continue working through hard times, and remain dedicated even when it feels like what you are doing is not working or you are not growing.

Developing mental toughness is entirely around being unwilling and unrelenting in the success that you desire to create. If you want to become mentally tough, you need to decide that you are going to stay committed to your goal no matter what that looks like and then show up every single day and put in the work necessary to move you closer to your goal. When you experience moments that feel challenging or that are trying on your emotions or your willingness to move forward, you need to be willing to give yourself five minutes or one day to have a self-pity party and then show up and move forward anyway. If you need to, look at yourself in the mirror and remind yourself why you are doing this and what attracted you to the idea of running your own business in the first place and continue talking to yourself until your passion and inner flame is respired so that you feel ready to move forward regardless of what anyone else says.

Staying Self-Motivated

One thing that most people are not prepared for when it comes to launching a business of their own is how much self-motivation is required in order to continue forward and create success in your personal business. In a business of your own, no one is going to stand over you and force you to work because, to put it simply, no one truly cares if you succeed or not unless you care. If you are committed to generating your own results, people will show up and be willing to lead you through the lessons that you need to learn in order to have the right skills to succeed. If you are not committed, people are going to recognize this and they are going to ignore you and your business and allow you to fail because it seems that this is where you are willing to end up.

Having self-motivation in your network marketing business means that you wake up every morning ready to find ways to show up and market to your audience and share with your followers. Self-motivation means that you reach out to your clients to do follow-ups and that you do what you can to get your hands on the resources that you need in order to learn more about your business and how you can create success with it. You need to be willing to step into the responsibility of learning what you need to learn in order to generate the success you want, otherwise, you are not going to be successful in your business at all. Remember, the only person who truly cares about your success is you. Everyone else trusts that the people who are ready to succeed will show up and then they are ready to commit to teaching *those* people because they know that this is where their energy will be best invested.

Stay Curious

Curiosity is a powerful emotion that can inspire you to continue learning, researching, and growing both as a person and as a network marketer. If you want to develop your mindset in a powerful way, learn to stay curious and ask questions from a place of curiosity rather than a place of expectation. Staying curious can support you in detaching from the outcome and moving into an emotional state of being open to what might happen for you, which means that you are focused on having what you desire or something better. It also allows you to stay emotionally open to receiving feedback and guidance so that, should you find that you are not creating the results that you desire, you are open to listening to why and finding new ways to start doing better in your business.

When it comes to staying curious, the best thing that you can do is to learn how to replace your fear with curiosity so that you can start looking for new answers and opportunities. The easiest way to do this is through reframing or looking at your fears from a new perspective so that they no longer seem as frightening. For example, if you are afraid of experiencing rejection so you worry about making offers to people or you feel anxious anytime you enter a prospective sales call with a potential customer, you may be emphasizing on your fear of rejection. Instead, pay attention to the curious side of you. Get curious about what the other person may want or need, how you may be able to support them, or why they were uninterested in your offer if they do reject you. When you come from a mindset of curiosity, you come prepared to learn and grow which means that your success becomes inevitable.

Monitor Your Thoughts

Our thoughts have a major impact on our ability to generate success because they can lead to us feeling, acting, and behaving in different ways depending on what our thoughts are. If you are struggling to generate success in your life, chances are you are holding onto thoughts that suggest that you are incapable or inferior and therefore you are unable to generate the energy or willingness to move forward and become successful in your business. If you are not self-disciplined with your thoughts, they can truly lead to personal sabotage and destruction quickly.

When you start growing your business, set the intention to start monitoring your thoughts and taking control over the many ways that they may be preventing you from going forward and generating the success that you desire. When you do, you may find that you were thinking thoughts that lead to you feeling less than you are, or like you are unworthy or undeserving of generating the success that you desire. You may also find yourself repeating things like "I can't" or "I won't" or "I'm not lucky" in your mind, all of which can lead to you feeling incompetent and emotionally unwilling to put yourself out there and generate the results that you desire in your life.

In order to start adjusting your thoughts, you need to be willing to believe that the thoughts that you are thinking to yourself are untrue. If you believe that they are true, it will be harder for you to accept them as false and move forward without them. You can begin to shift your beliefs by debunking your thoughts or challenging them, thus allowing you to see how false they are and what you can do to shift yourself into a new way of thinking. For example, say you have the belief that you are not lucky enough to be able to generate the success that you desire in your business so you believe that you will never become successful. Instead of holding onto that belief, start challenging it by looking at the people who you believe are successful and paying attention to what they did that actually made them successful. I guarantee that every single person will claim that luck had little to nothing to do with it and that they generated or maintained their success through their own efforts and actions.

Once you have challenged the thoughts, you need to replace them with new thoughts that are more inspiring and uplifting. For example, thoughts like "I can," "I will learn," or "I will." These types of positive and inspiring thoughts will support you in feeling more confident in being able to generate the success you desire in your life. The more you think these thoughts, the easier it will be for you to feel confident in your ability to create your desired reality and generate success in your life. Your self-esteem will increase, your stamina will increase, and your mental toughness will increase when you start thinking affirming thoughts. All of these positive shifts in your life will not only support you in feeling more capable and confident in building your own business, but they will also reflect in how you show up and share your business with others, which will result in you generating more success overall.

Chapter 10: Future of Network Marketing

There is no way to guarantee what will happen in the future, but one thing is fairly certain — network marketing is not going anywhere any time soon. To date, network marketing has made more millionaires than any other industry which means that more people are looking to get involved in these models and try them out to see if they themselves can become the next self-made millionaire through network marketing. In fact, network marketing has become so popular that many companies who previously sold their products online or in stores have shifted into using network marketing models so that they can get in front of more people and generate more sales.

When it comes to retail companies building their businesses, network marketing is a great way to grow faster and get in front of more people without having to do quite so much themselves. Instead of having to allot a budget to marketing and advertising and hiring a team of people to do it for them, companies can simply recruit network marketers and have these consultants do all of the marketing for them while getting paid commissions in return. Then, all the company needs to do is generate marketing materials for those consultants to purchase and use and generate the products for those consultants to sell. Otherwise, the entire marketing and sales departments of their companies have been outsourced and they do not have to do anything to get their company out there.

Because network marketing is highly effective and risk-free for everyone involved, many people are continually getting on board with this business model and generating some level of success for themselves. This means that it is likely that more businesses will convert to this business model and more people will choose to join so that they can work toward generating success with the new venture. One extremely positive thing about network marketing is that many people are thrilled with the model itself and want to take advantage of it to start generating money so even if they have had a failed experience in the past, many would be willing to try again if they were joining the right team and company. The fact that so many people are willing to rejoin or try again even if they have not yet generated success in the past is evidence that network marketing is a positive and powerful tool and that many people see the benefit of this business model.

Another reason why network marketing is likely to continue growing and evolving is because we have begun connecting in such a massive way through social media and the internet in general. Since network marketing largely relies on having a network, and social media is largely based on connecting networks regardless of borders, the two works together incredibly well to start generating more success for each party involved. When you start network marketing, one of your biggest growth opportunities will likely be social media since you can grow faster and reach more people this way. As you start to grow more on social media, generating more sales through this platform becomes easier as well because people start recognizing you and paying attention to what you are offering.

The addition of social media to network marketing has also reinforced the power of social proof, which is a marketing aspect that many companies leverage in order to grow their businesses. Social proof essentially highlights peoples' desire to purchase things only after they have seen other people effectively use and fall in love with these products and continue using them. When people see others using products and loving them, they can trust that they will likely fall in love with the products as well, which encourages them to purchase the products to try for themselves. This is why affiliate marketing is growing in popularity as we speak because people begin to trust the affiliate marketers and when the individual promotes a product they can trust that they will like the product too, so they try it.

As a network marketer, you are leveraging the power of social proof by building a network of people who trust in you and in what you promote and by promoting the products that you think your audience will like the most. The more you use these products and your audience uses the products and raves about how great they are, the more the rest of your audience is going to see just how powerful these products are and why they need to start using them as well. As you continue to generate more attention by having more people agree that the products rock, you will have more people joining you and wanting to purchase from you, which means that your company grows. Both companies and wise consultants know about the power of social proof which is why they opt to lean into this business model because it works.

The future of network marketing looks highly promising based on the nature of marketing trends and the way that the digital world is going. If you are looking for a lucrative business opportunity that is going to be here to stay, getting involved in network marketing is a great idea. While no one can predict the future, there is a good chance that network marketing will only continue to evolve and grow in popularity as more people see how valuable it is and start making their own success from this business model.

Conclusion

Congratulations on completing *Network Marketing Success!*

I hope that through reading this book, you are feeling more confident than ever before in your ability to leverage the network marketing business model so that you can start having greater success in your industry. Network marketing is a powerful business model that provides people with an easy way to begin generating financial freedom through the power of their own efforts. If you are interested in network marketing or if you have already joined with a company, I hope that following the guidance in this book will support you in generating the successful results that you desire to create in your business.

Devoting yourself to a company and promoting it like it is your own can be a tiresome job, particularly if you are not entirely sure about how to approach your business. You may encounter many naysayers and people who believe that you will not be able to make it work, but you need to reinforce yourself through your own mental toughness and desire to succeed and use that to achieve the success that you desire. The more you practice and stay invested in making your dreams come true, the easier it will be for you to make consistent progress every single day.

After you read this book, it is important that you audit where you are presently at in your business venture as a network marketer and start applying the strategies that you have learned right here in this book. If you have not yet started with a company, start from the very beginning of this book and follow the steps required to help you ensure that you join with the right company for you. If you have already joined but you are brand new, or if you have joined but you are not yet generating the traction that you desire, read through the marketing and mindset strategies in this book and use them to start generating greater success in your business. Make sure that you keep this book handy too so that you can access these resources again as needed, to help you generate even more success in your business.

Lastly, if you felt that the book *Network Marketing Success* supported you in generating success in your own business, or in providing you with knowledge on how to generate more success, please consider reviewing it on Amazon Kindle. Your honest feedback would be greatly appreciated, as it will support myself in generating more great content for you and others in gaining access to this valuable information so that everyone can succeed. Thank you.

www.ingramcontent.com/pod-product-compliance
Lightning Source LLC
Chambersburg PA
CBHW071259220526
45468CB00001B/194